SIX
FIGURE
SUCCESS
SECRETS

VOLUME 1

Cover by Daniel McCutcheon

For Cover Art Inquiries Contact mccutcheondan@gmail.com

1st Edition

Table of Contents

Introduction

There's no one right way to build a successful and thriving business. In this book, you'll hear from 8 entrepreneurs who've built extraordinary businesses, all in unique ways. You don't have to conform to someone else's ideals around creating a business; you get to build yours your way!

These entrepreneurs have dedicated themselves to serving others. Each has faced big fears, embraced personal growth, and leaped bravely into the unknown, all so they could tap into their full potential. Entrepreneurship isn't for the faint of heart, yet it can be one of the most fulfilling roads to travel.

You'll also see where there is overlap in these author's journeys because, ultimately, success leaves tangible clues. Study their success, and you will see the thread that weaves its way through each path. Enjoy!

Nicole Cherie Hesse

Every Little Girl Should Have a Unicorn

Remember wanting that pony *so bad* when you were little? You spent hours imagining what it would feel like to have your hair whipping in the wind as the hooves of this majestic animal thundered against the earth beneath you, all while you were carried off into the wild world of the unknown. Our dreams of freedom begin long before most of us know the burdens of what adulthood has in store for us.

Being a child is magical, with each day full of wonder, *even* if that childhood is riddled with the real-life monsters that go bump in the night like mine was. Despite what I endured, somehow, my imagination remains intact. My childlike wonder still exists, stubbornly growing like a flower pushing its way up through inhospitable concrete. I found a way to keep the sparkle in my eye through the abuse. My precocious little mind expanded beyond the edges of what seems possible when I look back at it now.

I was published for the first time when I was five; it was a poem about a unicorn in a meadow. The book had a brown, gritty cover, and I can still remember my mom flipping to the page my poem was printed on and showing me my name. I clearly remember the scent of the pages as if I could smell the printing press that birthed them. I can vividly recall the sound of the crinkling of the corners of the pages and the feeling of warmly being wrapped in my mother's supportive arms.

I always had big dreams. Dreams of being an author, a marine biologist, a lawyer… or maybe just running away into the forest and discovering that unicorns really are real. My 7-year-old self painted a picture that stretched beyond what the eye could see so that all the dark parts were just swallowed up. My mind became vast in its expression, like an ocean, impervious to the dark and twisted creatures swimming in the deep.

That kind of capacity would be hard to believe in now if it weren't for the vantage point of watching my own daughter. She shows me each and every day that we are, in fact, limitless; the rules, the struggles, and the boxes we get restricted within are all self-imposed. We *learn* to cage ourselves in. We *learn* to choose fear and suffering. We give up the ponies and dreams and trade them for societal norms and the status quo, all in the pursuit of this thing we call *belonging*. Ironically enough, in this quest to fit in, we so often brush aside the very things that make us special. The magic itself curls up like a yawning baby dragon and may lay dormant inside us for decades, if not forever, if never reawakened.

We finish school. We get jobs. We do what we are supposed to do. Pretending to be a part of the well-oiled machine that we call society. We assimilate. We fall in line. We fall in love. We climb corporate ladders. We buy insurance and become adults, whatever the hell that means, and for what? To earn the respect of the other robots? If you stop and think about it, it really doesn't make any sense at all. Seeking the approval of the ambiguous "they," trying desperately to be successful as if a certificate will show up in the mail proclaiming that you have finally reached success status. We endure all of that struggle, strife, and endless rat-racing exhaustion just to prove to the eye in the sky that we are good humans deserving of the gold star of mediocrity.

We push our pennies together and make a decent living to keep a roof over our heads and have pretty pictures on our Instagram accounts. We smile for the selfies and swipe right to filter our faces and hide the flaws that are all we have left of actually being able to relate to another human being to try to quell the agonizing longing to feel accepted by a world that scrolls right on by. The emptiness expands, and the cold dead hand of apathy sucks us into a vortex of reality TV and TikTok trends as the world wages war on sanity itself. But... *It doesn't have to be like this.*

Today, I share the story of just what happened when that sleeping baby dragon inside of me woke the fuck up, ravenous and rampaging. Mercilessly, she spit fire and burned down my whole damn life. It was a Tuesday, like any other. The road swerved out in front of me, dawn breaking, as I drove home from somewhere I never should have been. The robotic thought pattern continued to play on regretful repeat in my mind, as it always did. The sun sparkled over the ridge, and the same radiating thought tapped its way into my consciousness again, "I can't live like this anymore."

After dragging myself day by day through a decade of suicidal tendencies, backed up by two trips to the hospital and followed up by weeks in cold, sterile, little white rooms, the thought was nothing new. I was prepared to numbingly ignore it as I had done many times before, knowing that a shot of whiskey would soon follow and take away all the pain of being a unicorn trapped in the rotting flesh of an anxiety-ridden human. But that day, for no apparent rhyme or reason, was the day that everything changed. As the record swirled around beneath the arc of the needle, singing the same song yet again, "I can't live like this anymore," something incredible happened. A booming voice, the voice of that baby dragon, raspy and thirsty for the satisfaction of being seen and heard, simply replied to my recurring thought, "So don't."

Now, let's be clear - this won't seem incredible to you, and it doesn't seem incredible to me now because I know exactly what it was in hindsight that created this shift. However, I implore you to remember that all science was once seen as magic before we had the perspective to put circumstances into graphs, charts, and textbooks and call them facts.

It was in that exact moment that my whole world changed. I didn't know it then, but I sure as hell know it now as I *tip-tap-type* to you from my mansion on the hill overlooking the city, far away from where I used to live and who I used to be. Millions of dollars have been made since that moment, which really was not all that long ago. Sometimes, it's hard for me to believe just how fast it all happened as I went from a drunken, drowning mess of depression to a thought-leading wild unicorn on a mission filled with light and hope; all the things that my past self certainly would have rolled her eyes at. Yet, here I am, married to the love of my life, living in my dream home, hanging out with my two teenage kids, loving my life, and running my multi-7-figure business that helps other sleeping dragons to wake the fuck up and bring back the magic of life.

The day that my sleeping dragon woke up and took the wheel, simply suggesting that I stop living the way that I was living, was the day that I quit drinking cold turkey: no more cocaine, no more Jameson, no more one-night stands, and no more self-sabotage shenanigans. By the time I got home, I was a different person because it didn't take time to change, only intention. In that moment, a new thought was born, and a new feeling followed that new thought, and that new feeling led to a completely different course of action that yielded mind-blowing results. You can get the full story about this on my podcast, *Real Unicorns Don't Wear Pants*, but today, we are here to talk about one simple thing: how to wake up the dragon within you, also known as your higher self.

You see, at some point in our lives, we start believing that other people know best, and that we aren't real adults. We feel like we should just go along with the status quo to get by and that everyone else has access to some set of secret instructions for this thing called life. It's as if we were somehow absent from class that day, maybe at the dentist, when the teacher handed out the owner's manual to being a successful human. Slowly, eventually, through terrifying trials and tribulations, we begin to realize the horrifying truth: *we are the adults*, and no one actually knows what the fuck is going on. Need proof of this? Just become a mother and watch your teenage son attend high school classes where your sophomore-year boyfriend is the teacher. That will smack shit into perspective quickly.

We are the grownups. Scary right? Time bends, lightning strikes, and the dragon nods at you with that knowing smirk whispering, "I told you so," as you desperately rock back and forth, telling yourself that this is all a nightmare and you will wake up soon. At first, it's a devastating realization. Your Hogwarts letter isn't coming in the mail, and your parents don't have it all figured out. Not only do you have to grow up, but you already *are* a grown-up, and no one is coming to save you. This is life. You have arrived. The job you have, the spouse, and the house - you chose. Happy or not, this is what it is.

After awakening to this idea, you start to surrender to the idea that maybe you will just spend the next thirty years trying to figure out what you will cook for dinner, and the world goes gray in a haze. For most of us, this is the end of the story. Sure, they keep living, but there is nothing left to tell. The same day repeats over and over again until their inevitable end.

For a precious few of us, there is a plot twist, true to the story arc formula - right at the opportune moment, an unexpected turn of events changes everything. Your higher self shows up, guns blazing, ready to risk it all to save you from your stupid self and the life of mediocrity you'd otherwise keep living. The problem is, when this miraculous moment arrives, most people just lean back into their Lazy Boy, open the Facebook app, and change the channel. That spark of a brilliant idea that they had over dinner fades away into the stardust of self-doubt. The dream slithers back into the pipe, and most people wake up the next day and do exactly what they did yesterday, waiting for their gold star to arrive in the mail.

The cold, hard fact is that they don't call it the 1% for nothing. We need 99% of people to wake up tomorrow and do it all again. People living life like it's the *Groundhog Day* film keep the DMV running and food on the shelves at the supermarket. It's necessary. Most of the dragons need to just keep sleeping in order for society to keep on keeping on. But 1% is still a fuck-ton of people if you do the math. So, let me ask you a question: why not you? You are sitting here reading a book. Do you have any idea how rare that is in the first place? No one reads anymore, and you aren't just reading any book. You are reading a book filled with the magical energy of stories of success and fulfillment. Why did you pick this book up in the first place? Who are you really?

Sit still for just a second, and breathe deeply, all the way in, and all the way out. Can you hear it? That dragon of yours? Maybe she is still sleeping, like a house cat, with a soft rumble of a snore. Did you know that dragons purr? Well, they do. The fact is that there's potential inside of you that is inside of all of us. We are all beautiful, brilliant, sentient beings oozing with limitless capabilities, just waiting to be awakened. The problem is we have all been hit with a heavy dose of sleeping pills in the form of dreaded self-doubt. Even if the dragon does stir, dreaming of a better life, it is met with a swift kick from the naysayers:

"What makes you think that will work?"
"Ya right, in your dreams."
"Oh, my uncle tried that. Now he's bankrupt."

"Who do you think you are?"

The system is designed to keep you safely behaving in the exact same pattern as everyone else so that the status quo is never challenged, keeping society as we know it remaining exactly the same. The infamous "they" are betting on your self-doubt to keep you in line. They are capitalizing on your fear so that you stay comfortable while commuting to that 9-to-5 job, where you will make $26 an hour with your Ph.D. like a good little human.

We weren't born afraid, we are taught to be afraid, and to fall in line. We are graded on a curve through standardized tests and told that we are a whole lot prettier when we smile, and are seen but not heard. We are programmed for compliance. Then, after years of conditioning, we are willingly led to slaughter night after night, binging on Netflix, hopelessly distracted so as not to access the infinite amount of knowledge that we could acquire in a single night of online education.

Before you start asking me where I bought my tin foil hat, I want you to just take a moment to allow your mind to expand and remember what it was like to be seven years old. When I was seven, I was sitting on the couch, staring out the window, crying because my deadbeat dad wasn't coming to my birthday party. My mom held me tight and wiped away my tears, but never my fear of abandonment. I like to imagine a scenario where the current version of me, the fulfilled and successful me, is pulling up to my mom's house in my unicorn-white Bentley for that birthday party. Seven-year-old me smiles and runs outside to hug me because I showed up for her. She gets to see who I have become. She runs her fingers through my now silver hair and calls it my unicorn hair, just like my daughter does.

I really wish that 7-year-old me could meet my kids. Who knows? Maybe she did see me, maybe time rippled for just a moment, and she caught a glimpse of who she would become, and that's what helped her to get up and tell the judge in court that she didn't want to see the man who hit her mother anymore. Maybe in that moment when I hugged her, she gained enough strength to grow up and survive two more rapes and the death of her son's father. Maybe my 7-year-old self saw the wonder in my wild eyes and used that certainty to struggle through the ten years of depression and the death of her best friend, knowing that someday, she would become me, knowing that it would all eventually be worth it. Maybe 7-year-old me set the alarm clock for that sleeping dragon, and maybe it was her voice that said, "So don't."

While I may never know you, I can tell you that from where I sit now, high on the hill, that fulfillment finds us in the strangest ways. It is up to us to learn, listen, and choose to believe that voice inside of us. It is up to us to learn to heed the dragon and slay the self-doubt. It is up to us to make our 7-year-old selves proud. It is up to us to change the way we think and feel about ourselves so that we can master the art of painting our own picture of what this life is supposed to look like. When we do, that is when the magic comes flooding back.

When we learn to take radical responsibility for the questions that we ask ourselves every day, when we finally allow that dragon to spread its wings and carry us to where we want to go, and when we break free from who we were yesterday and choose to become the next version of ourselves, *that* is when we can access incredible results: 1% results. When I let go of the notion that I had to be who I used to be, that's when everything changed. That is when I stopped making the same choices. When I started doing things differently. When I started actually listening to myself instead of other people. I went from horribly abusive relationships that mirrored my monster of a father, to attracting a wonderful man, who is stored in my phone as *Daniel the Dragon.* We have the running joke that I made him out of clay. We met on a dating app, he left his state job, and we moved in together. He proposed in Santorini, and he just brought me a mac n' cheese brisket burrito while I finish this chapter for you. His eyes are golden green, and when I curl up next to him, I can hear his heart beating; he is everything I want in a husband. He smells like fulfillment. He is tangible proof of the person I have become, reflected right back to me through adoring eyes and a string of inside joke text messages. *He sends the best memes.*

When I started taking different actions in my life, I got fired from two bartender jobs in the same month. At the time, it was terrifying, but really, this was the furious wings of alignment carrying me to my true calling. From the ashes of bartender land, *Wonder World* emerged. I built a coaching empire, stampeding with unicorn clients. I crushed 7-figures in my first 13 months as a *Client Attraction Coach.* By modeling my methods of combining mindset with strategy into actionable steps to scale businesses, more millionaires have been born. It's working because each and every day, I get to wake up and play ponies with my friends on the internet, all while making 6-figures a month and helping others to do the same. It's pure, limitless magic. It's real, like I always knew it was when I was a little kid. Today, I know my 7-year-old self is smirking, because she told me so.

So, let me ask you again - do you remember wanting that pony so badly when you were little? Well, really, what's stopping you from getting it now that you are an adult? Seven-year-old me can tell you that it's only your self-doubt and your need to belong standing in your way. I'll let you in on a little secret… You already do belong. Separation is the illusion. We are the ones painting the picture, and we get to make up our own rules, which can be terrifying at first, but once you choose to embody your true power to create the results you want in your life, you will unlock your limitless potential.

Here's the million-dollar question... *How do you wake up the dragon?* Simply by believing that there is one sleeping on your chest right now.

Believing is seeing.

Wake up.

Richard Blakely

I started my I.T. company over 32 years ago with $500 to my name, 30 days to make the rent, and my wife and I had a 3-year-old baby ta-boot. I jumped straight to the deep end, and then learned how to swim.

Although I had experience working for large corporations in my field, in the three years prior to starting my own business, I worked for two smaller companies in a row whose philosophy was solely money-driven, and it drove me crazy. I watched those business owners lie and price gouge their customers at almost every turn, providing poor products, high prices, slow service, and hitting them with big bills. It was always about money, the bottom line, the take home, and themselves.

I am just not built that way. I am and have always been an honest person. If you ask me a question, you'll get the truth, whether you like it or not, but it's always the truth. Much to the chagrin of both of those business owners, if a customer asked me a question, they got the truth, even if it bit me in the ass with a mad boss. Like I said, I'm not built to lie; it's not me, not who I am.

During those three years with those two bosses, I saw what not to do, which was massively valuable. I'd had enough of shyster number one, who, when hiring me, had *faked* an accent (if you can believe that) to make me feel more at home, then lowballed my salary offer. He also lied on my tax slips that year and left me holding the bag for a large tax bill (this gives you an idea of who he was), so I paid the bill and never looked back. I should have seen the writing on that wall, but sometimes we don't. Everyone has something to teach us, so I resigned and moved on.

Shyster number two was a god in his own mind, and he was no better. He pushed me to try and pilfer the clients from the previous business

I'd worked for. He didn't want to pay gas mileage costs even though I drove my own car, and he thought cold calling was the way to riches; it's not. Don't cold call. What a waste of time. Given what he was doing to clients, I was almost at the point of not sleeping, and I just could not keep working there. Within nine months, I was heading out that door. After a long weekend of thinking, I decided it was time to go out on my own, bust or boom, because the one thing I do know is that I can rely on myself.

I did some research and quickly realized the town we lived in was just not going to support us. It was too small and spread out, and driving from town to town would not work, eating up most of my time driving. We found a small city that worked for our family and for what I do, and we moved. Adaptation is important. Why try to sell cars in a town that only uses public transit or sell baby products to a seniors' center? If something does not make sense, make a change.

By moving, we changed the location to fit the skill. You must be willing to make changes to make it work, and most people won't need to move. Still, change, any change, also means flexibility – be flexible and adapt like a chameleon that takes on its environment, and stop banging your head against the wall because things don't line up the way *you* wanted or thought they should. Allow yourself to be wrong, then own it.

Allow yourself to be wrong, then own it.

If you've read some "Start your own Business" books, you've most likely read the common things that people believe businesses are: how to "make it big," "be your own boss," yada-yada... forget all that. Let these preconceptions go; after all, they aren't your ideas of what business might or should be like, but they're other people's ideas. Whose business is it anyway, theirs or yours?

The cold, hard, and delightful facts are that anyone can open a business with a permit and a hundred bucks, but if you are in it to get rich quick, want to take regular 3-day weekends, and slide into the office frequently at 9:30 because you own the joint, then please, stick to your day job. Running a business takes a lot of commitment, time, and effort to get it off the ground, and money needs to be the last thing on your mind; it was when I started, and still is, the least important part of my day.

If you have a good marketable skill or an idea to fill a need in your area, something lacking in the marketplace, and you can fill that black hole, or if you can just do something already offered *way* better than the three other companies doing it now half-heartedly, then excellent, you are off to a good start. I can't help you much there, *you* need to figure this one out all on your own, but make sure you choose something that makes you happy, you *want* to enjoy going to work, and look forward to it so that in 5 years you won't hate it; long term thinking, but it's important to start on the right foot.

My company is a company built on customer-first service, and our product is knowledge and know-how. If you picked out the key part of the previous sentence right away, then you definitely have the right mindset to succeed.

Customer-First Service.

Let me tell you the basic things that work for me that I've gleaned and implemented, and that should work for any business owner, that will put you onto the path to success:

➤ Listen – your customers will always tell you what they want, but you must listen to hear them. No one ever learned anything by talking, so get over yourself, shut up, and listen. You'll be glad you did.

➤ Tell them the truth, always. If you say, "I don't know," that's OK, I say it still, but to succeed, you MUST always follow up with, "But I'll find out and get back to you," and oh baby, you MUST follow through in a timely manner - MUST – you are building a reputation here so EARN IT!

➤ Whatever you sell, be it products or services, make them the best. I don't and won't sell cheap products. Sure, this can lead to a quick sale, which can be initially tempting, but long-term, poor quality is remembered indefinitely after the sale and negates repeat purchases, good reviews, or referrals. Don't do it, and just say NO; reputation is everything.

  ○ TID-BIT: Many years ago, early on, a client we had for about three years convinced me they were opening a branch office and needed a "really cheap computer" just to get the branch started. Initially, I pushed back some and asked them repeatedly to add an upgraded warranty to be safe, but he was persistent and emphatic it was all they wanted, and I relented and got him what he asked for. Inevitably, the machine didn't last well, as it was nothing like all the other machines I'd provided, but it was exactly what he asked for and did the job initially. In the end, I had to let that client go over it two years later; he just never stopped talking about how poor it was, and somehow, it was my fault he insisted on a cheap one. Got it, lesson learned.

➤ Forget the money – no, really. If all you think about is money, then become a banker. It's not lost on me that we need money to eat, pay rent, buy clothes, and get around, but this is not, and should never be, a business focus. If you visit the Fortune 500 companies and read every one of their Corporate Statements about who they are, not one of them says, "We're in it for the money."

➤ There is no nine to five in business land – be ready to work, a lot, and work I did, service calls all day, orders end of day, paperwork and estimates till 2 am, accounting on Saturdays (hey, just one of me and all hats fit in the early days) then repeat, and 80-hour work weeks happened, a lot. You need to put in the effort in the beginning to get this off the ground. Then you can hire, delegate, and bring life back to balance, but be ready to give it everything. Would I do this again? You're damn right I would – and It IS worth it. You'll remember I mentioned we had a three-year-old, and she got my every lunch hour, early morning, and supper time. I rarely missed a night to tuck in and read a story – this was critically important to me, and her. There's always time for both.

➢ I learned to do everything and then taught others. I never wanted to be beholden to any employee where I needed their skill, but no one else in the company could do it. This can lead to the staff holding you hostage one day by leaving unexpectedly or forcing a pay raise you can't refuse to finish a project commitment. Obviously, it's not feasible in every business model for you to personally know how to do everything, but in those cases, hedge your bets. When hiring, cross-hire employees where skills cross each other, so Susan can do Phil's job competently if Phil leaves – for example. You need to always be the decider. It's your company, your vision, so listen, learn, and invite comments, yes, but be the decision maker and lead them to bigger and better things.

➤ Share the wealth – I believe in sharing a company's success with the people who make it happen every day, the employees, contractors, etc. With good living wages, flexible work hours, and equal pay, everyone wins, or no one does. This philosophy pays dividends you can only dream of and, in the end, costs you nothing.

➤ Hit the street – remember, cold calling, in my opinion, is a failed strategy. Go and talk to people in person, face to face, have some basic info in hand, ASK for an opportunity, and follow up with a second visit in 7-10 days. When I started out, we hit businesses when we were not busy, and we were not busy A LOT in the beginning, so I talked to many folks, and a good percentage of them tried us out when their current supplier, inevitably, let them down. That's all I needed: one, and the foot was in the door, and quality products and services sell themselves.

○ TID-BIT - We often hear of many businesses going under. Do you ever wonder why? Was it the box store that moved in, the economy, the pandemic, or the weather? A hard no to all of these things; it was the business owner's failure to adapt, to change, to keep driving forward, and to maintain quality and integrity.

➤ Goals are essential as you build your business, and they are mutable and changing, just like your clients' needs are. I set a monthly goal for gross revenue (NOTE - I'm using this as a measuring stick for business expansion/ growth and not as a "look at the money we earned" – these are different animals altogether), and surprisingly, I reached it in under a year. When I set the goal, it seemed lofty, not silly, unachievable, but a bit of a stretch, and I worked for it and got there. Then I set another, and another - and as I reached each of them, I realized I was forcing myself to become more creative, to learn different income streams, and to expand my business in ways I had not thought of in the beginning. Set goals, work toward them, and if they stall, look for alternate ways to get there; offer a different service, companion selling, find the need you are not filling, and fill it. This brings me to an important topic: face time – no, not the app, but customer face time, where you go and say hello in person. With regular visits, by either doing some of the service work, delivering a product order, or just dropping in, you'll notice (if you keep your eyes and ears open, that is) that clients are showing you what they need and will tell you what they want, even if it's a competitor's box on the floor for a product you don't offer – and should be. Client face time also keeps you at the top of the client's mind, and top of mind means you are the first one they call or email when they need your services; be the one they think of first.

➤ But what about the money!? Okay, okay, it's simple, really simple. If you focus on and only provide quality products and services each time, every time, you won't have to think about money. Why? Because money, simply put, is a natural by-product of good quality products and services. Low product returns (almost zero), doing the job right, every time, and if something happens (yes, shit happens, who knew?), <u>making it right</u>, every time – and those clients won't go anywhere. Customers do understand you are human and that we make mistakes or have bad days; it happens. What separates you as a business owner from the others, is that you own it, you correct it, and you make it right. Sometimes you have to (or want to) suck up the costs, but hey, it <u>was your mistake,</u> so think of it as on-the-job training expenses. Fixing it now and owning it pays dividends in terms of loyalty, word-of-mouth referrals, and good will. In fact, those clients will tell their clients (and friends, neighbors, and associates) about you! Yes, about your error, but most importantly, how well you took care of THEM, reinforcing their good choice in choosing you. Repeat after me, "Money takes care of itself." Now, forget about it.

○ TID-BIT - Almost 34 years later, we still have our first client as a customer. You can't buy that kind of loyalty – but you can damn well earn it. Make it happen.

➤ When your corporate rock and roll finds its groove, you'll be silly busy, but in a great way. You'll stop one day and realize, "Wow, I'm here, the place I always wanted to be," and kudos to you – it's a long but satisfying road. Now what? If you have not given it any thought before, you should do it now. Do you want to keep growing, expanding, adding employees (joys and headaches) and become a blue-chip stock, multi million-dollar multinational – or not? Personally, I had no interest in that kind of more - more time commitments (less time for you/family), more problems, and less customer face time. Success is a measurement that has many yardsticks: wealth, power, awards, achievement, and so on. For me, success was bringing up a child and giving her all the time I possibly could (there's never enough, I can promise you, and it's now or never – kids grow up fast), paying off our house mortgage, quality vacation time and squeezing in some me time. Success was about having a nice cushion in the bank, a good, reliable car, a rainy-day fund, and paying for our girl's tuition so she didn't have to work and could go to University. Planning for and affording a well-earned retirement is also a goal, including travel, fun, and family. So, take the time to define where your road leads from this place, where you want to end up, and when you want to arrive there. When the time comes to walk away and retire, you'll be ready.

➤ Eggs and baskets – many businesses end up with some large contracts that generate a large portion of the corporate revenue – awesome – but deadly. I'm not suggesting you don't take that contract, but if you're not careful, all your eggs can end up in one basket, and then you're in trouble. I can relay my experience. We landed a large multi-state company's contract for offices in several cities within a 90-minute drive of our office. On top of that, we had already gotten a foot in the door at a company that had offices in many of the same towns this new contract was covering – hey, WIN-WIN. As we improved and expanded our large client, we got more and more work from the "third party" supplier for their client base – and before we knew it, these two alone were 80% of our revenue. It snuck up on me; we were busy, growing, and doing well, but I sat and did some numbers one day and was taken aback by how much these two have taken over. Large corporate or third-party suppliers can be very fickle and can drop you and move for a better price in a heartbeat, and out the door sails a large portion of your revenue, then employee layoffs, and it's all a clawback from there. Once I saw the numbers, I stopped and refocused on diversifying back out to smaller clients and made that the push. We grew the small business market well over time, and then the third party bailed for a cheaper contractor (this turned out to be a really good thing) – but we were ready and had replaced their workload in only months. Next, the large corporation we'd been servicing outsourced more, and off that went to a multinational contractor – but we were ready. We were able to replace that income as well in a reasonable time. Now, our largest client only represents 5% of our revenue stream, and it's a nice, comfortable place to be – this is what you are looking for, many eggs, many baskets.

➤ You need to fire a client now and then. Yes, it seems inconceivable and counterintuitive, but I can assure you that it's needed. In the beginning, this seems crazy (the old mans flipped his wig) kind of crazy, and certainly, early on, some bending is in order to get to know a client, but you'll get here faster than you think. Some clients, you know the ones, are frankly far more trouble than they are worth. They always want to save a buck, and they pay late, 45-60–90 days. Are you a bank? These are the clients that regularly call in the evenings, during dinner, on weekends, and on holidays. They just expect you to help them 24/7. They call, and if you don't answer, they call again over and over until you (frustrated now) finally pick up because THEY have a question (oh, it's not an emergency). Fire them – I mean it, let the poor-quality "chase the dollar" competition have them. They deserve them and will put up with them trying to make that extra buck, not realizing it's costing them two. Find and nurture clients who appreciate you, your work and respect you enough to pay on time., Great clients do call off hours sometimes, it happens; but these ones apologize out of the gate for calling after hours and ask kindly for assistance - it is an emergency, and that's the only reason they called - THOSE are keepers we look for. Now that you've found them, coddle them, love them, and treat them like family because these are the clients you have always dreamed of.

After your efforts, if you do this right, you will arrive at the place every business owner wants to be, but few obtain. This is the holy grail of business/client relationships. When you get here, you have arrived at the one position your competition cannot get to, and no matter how hard they try, they won't dislodge you from that mantle in your customers mind – the "Trusted Advisor." This takes several things, and of course, time.

The keys to this are simple yet effective. In everything you do, be:

- ✓ Consistent – quality matters, this time, every time.
- ✓ Persistent - follow through, follow up, no excuses.
- ✓ Integrity - honesty is the only policy.
- ✓ Service – how can I help you today? (even if you must offer a solution from others.)
- ✓ Excellence – accept nothing less from yourself and, by extension, from those you hire.

The first time a client asks you to weigh in on a problem, an issue, or even a personal matter that has absolutely nothing to do with what you do, you know you've arrived – you are now their Trusted Advisor. Bravo.

Final words

I could likely go on for hours, and I'm really not the chatty type either, about how the "banks" wanted us to put up 100% of the loan to guarantee a loan because we "didn't have a track record" – well fuck that! *If we had the money, we would not have needed the loan!* I have a lot of little things that took years to learn, but you will learn them; just be open to learning them. I still take regular courses online, read industry articles consistently, and continue to look for new skills for me and our clients. Take a leap of faith (in yourself), and you can do what you set your mind to, so do it. The rewards of starting and owning a business can be immeasurable. I tried and rejected being a corporate drone – it wasn't for me. I'm so glad I believed enough in myself to do it – scary, hell yes, and the road has not been without its bumps and bruises, but I've seen more dead bodies walk out of a 9-5 job than I care to count, I would not be one of them – and here I am, and I'd do it all over again.

Sarah Lines

"The journey of a thousand miles begins with one step."

-Lao Tzu

It was 2016, and I was 2-years clean and sober. The nursing board had paid to fly me to Sydney for a psychiatric evaluation to see if I was mentally fit enough to work again as a midwife. I'd passed all the drug and alcohol tests and was ready to join the "real" world again.

I was so thrilled to get that piece of paper in the mail to confirm I was re-registered! I felt like a worthwhile human being again. An asset to society instead of a leach. But something was gnawing at me from the inside, a persistent thought that would not let up, "I don't think I want this anymore."

One thing my recovery had taught me was that life was too short to waste it on being false. I realized that although I loved caring for people, a different path was calling to me, something much bigger than I could even perceive at the time. So, I decided to put my nursing career aside and become a *Reiki Healer.* This was the first breadcrumb from my soul, calling me down an unknown path and into service.

I opened up a healing room, and it felt nice, but I knew I wasn't going to stop there. I kept getting the nudge to go much bigger and to serve many people. I realized I had to take my business online, so I created a course for chakra clearing that offered a private healing experience. I was proud of myself, but I quickly discovered that I had zero idea how to market and sell!

This brought up a whole lot of stuff for me: "I'm not good enough to do this." "Who do I think I am?" "I don't deserve to be paid." Amidst this internal tailspin, I began the search for a mentor. I quickly found the perfect woman named Jen. She was a business kinesiologist and an entrepreneur alignment coach. We worked together for a couple of months, clearing all my emotional *stuff.* It was beautiful, and I loved the process, but at the end of it, I still had no idea how to run a business.

I invested most of the hours in my day into learning and researching how to run an effective online business. I did this learning despite my busy schedule, with my son who has special needs, and in between my part-time job and in-person clients. I was driven to make it work.

I invested in coach after healer, after psychic, after mentor, but despite all of the wisdom they imparted, something was holding me back from making money in my online business. It was me; *I knew it was me.* Even though I'd healed so much, I still had guilt about receiving and a strong block around being visible. I believed my services were not good enough for someone to want to exchange money for them, and I honestly just did not want to be seen.

I was desperately shy and hated going LIVE on camera. Yes, *hated.* But from all my research, I knew that live video was the way forward. It was during a past-life regression that I was able to clear my lack of confidence and visibility block. This one session would become the catalyst for everything else to start to fall into place, and it set me up for how I would work with women in the future.

I had become certified as a *Quantum Reiki Grandmaster* and a *Happiness Life Coach,* but my soul was still nudging me. I felt it in my bones. I had to create a global impact, and I had to do my part and fulfill my soul's mission here: helping in the ascension of our planet. *But what was my path?* That's where my beautiful Starseed family came through strong. I asked for guidance, and boy did I get it. I created a deep connection with the star people and asked them every day to show me the way to my highest path in this life. I asked them to help me live my purpose and stay on my path.

Sometimes, I received direct guidance telepathically from them. Other times, I would just intuitively know what I had to do. I kept following the nudges I felt deep within.

I was stepping through fear again and again. Honoring this path meant showing up live in front of people, even though I feared they would judge me and tell me I was wrong. It meant staying on track and continuing my business journey, even though a client might have left my world, or if I received hate messages from people. It meant rising continuously and up-leveling again and again. It meant shining brightly, even if this was triggering to others. I realized the more I did this, as painful as it was, the more soul-aligned people came into my world who loved me just as I am.

I moved through tragedy and triggers. I have a special needs child at home, who I homeschool, who does not sleep and has some full-on behavior issues. My husband has bipolar, and I experience extreme fatigue and cycling depression. Despite these hurdles, I never stop. I chose this life and will not leave until I have completed my mission here: to help as many people as possible awaken and ascend and create the life and business of their dreams. Good people do good things with money, so I'm determined to help them get their hands on more of it. The more heart-centered entrepreneurs I can help create to wild success, the better.

I'm here to pave the way to New Earth and help others do the same, creating a ripple effect across the planet. And I believe this is a big part of how I've come to own a 6-figure business.

I firmly believe you create success by living your purpose. You have probably heard the phrase, "Do what you love, and the money will follow." This is great advice, but not always easy to follow. It can be difficult to know what your purpose is, and even harder to align your occupation with your life's mission. However, it is possible to create success by living your purpose. Here's how:

1. Determine your values.

The first step is to get clear on your values. What is important to you? What do you believe in? Make a list. When you are living and working in alignment with your values, success will naturally follow.

2. Assess your skills and talents.

After you have determined your values, then take an inventory of your skills and talents. What are you good at? What do you enjoy doing? Consider how your skills and talents can be used in a way that aligns with your values. For example, if you value creativity and enjoy working with your hands, a career in art or design may be a good fit for you. If you have a hard time linking up your values to your skills, it's a great idea to consult a business coach to discuss the multitude of options.

3. Find a need and fill it.

In order for your business to be successful, you must find a need in the marketplace and fill it. This means offering a product or service that people want or need and are willing to pay for. When you are clear about what you have to offer and who you are offering it to, success will come more easily.

4. Be passionate about what you do.

Finally, remember to be passionate about what you do! If you are not passionate about your work, it will be hard to maintain long-term motivation. Find something that ignites a fire within you and go after it wholeheartedly. When you are living your purpose, success will be sure to follow.

Your purpose is what sets your heart on fire and gets you excited about life. It is what makes you feel most alive. When you are living your purpose, you feel like everything falls into place, and nothing can stop you. That is because when you are true to yourself, the universe conspires to support you.

If you believe you are in alignment with your purpose, and you've been taking consistent action over a reasonable period of time, but the money still isn't flowing, it might be time to reassess. You may have deep financial blocks that need to be cleared in order to achieve that next level. Maybe your goals and dreams have changed since you first started your business, and it's time to really sit with your soul and ask for guidance. Or perhaps you need to refine your sales and marketing skills. Whatever the case may be, trust your intuition to guide you to the right answer.

Society often tells us that success is defined by things like having a good job, a nice house, and a family. I believe that real success comes from living a life that is in alignment with who you are meant to be. So, what is true success for you? Take time to truly define this for yourself so that you don't waste any of your precious time on this earth building someone else's dream. If success to you truly includes creating a 6-figure business that you are in love with, then here are six essential secrets that every entrepreneur needs to know in order to achieve 6-figure success:

1. Focus on Your Strengths

One of the most important things you can do as an entrepreneur is to focus on your strengths. Identify what you're good at and build your business around that. Don't try to be everything to everyone; just be the best at what you do. When you focus on your strengths, you'll naturally attract clients who appreciate your unique talents and abilities.

2. Create a Compelling Vision

Another secret of 6-figure success is to have a compelling vision for your business. What is it that you want to achieve? What impact do you want to make in the world? When you can articulate a clear and inspiring vision for your business, it will give you the motivation and direction you need to overcome any obstacle and achieve any goal.

3. Set Powerful Goals

Setting goals is essential for any entrepreneur who wants to achieve 6-figure success. But not just any old goals will do; they must be *specific, measurable, attainable, relevant,* and *time-bound* (SMART). That means they should be clearly defined so that you know exactly what you need to do in order to achieve them. Having

SMART goals gives you a roadmap to success and keeps you focused on what's important.

4. Take Consistent Action

No matter how great your vision or how powerful your goals may be, they won't amount to anything if you don't act on them. Consistent action is the key to achieving any goal, including the goal of generating a 6-figure income. When you take consistent action towards your goals, even when you don't feel like it, eventually, those actions will start to pay off and lead to the success you desire.

5. Stay Positive Through Adversity

The road to success is never smooth; there will always be obstacles and challenges along the way. The key is not to allow those challenges to defeat you or derail your progress. Instead, stay positive and maintain faith in yourself and your ability to overcome whatever adversity comes your way. Remember, every challenge is an opportunity for growth and expansion if you face it with courage and persistence.

6. Get Help When You Need It

As an entrepreneur, there's nothing wrong with asking for help when you need it—in fact, it's one of the smartest things you can do! No one has all the answers or knows everything about every aspect of business; instead, we all have strengths and weaknesses. When you're faced with a challenge outside of your area of expertise or comfort zone, reach out for help from someone who has the knowledge and experience needed to help you solve the problem. And don't forget—there are many resources available online that can provide helpful information when you need it.

These are just a few of the secrets that every entrepreneur needs to know in order to achieve 6-figure success! By focusing on your strengths, setting SMART goals, taking consistent action towards those goals, staying positive through adversity, and getting help when needed, you'll be well on your way toward creating a successful business that generates income year after year!

Amy Dabrush Lewis

Adopt a Mindset of Relentless Growth and Evolution, and
For Goodness Sake Prioritize Yourself

Hey there! I'm Amy, and I'm so glad you've joined me here. Go ahead, grab a cuppa your favorite beverage, get comfortable, and let's explore what it really takes to achieve 6-figure success.

In order to achieve 6-figure success in business, first and foremost, *you'll want to adopt a mindset of relentless growth and evolution.* You'll need to be constantly learning new strategies and techniques, and then putting them into practice. Simultaneously, you'll be shedding layers of yourself to make room for your own evolution in mind and spirit as you rise, embrace your true self, and stand in your power to achieve everything you desire and more.

The best way to approach this chapter is to read it through in its entirety. Don't worry if not all the concepts make sense at first. You are sure to get what you need in this moment during your first read-through. When you return to this chapter repeatedly, rest assured you will also get new insights each time. I highly recommend grabbing a highlighter and/or a pen for taking notes and highlighting concepts that speak to you so that you can have reminders of where you want to focus.

In this chapter, I am honored to share with you a simple *3-Part System* I developed from my own experience and from working with my clients to help them achieve and exceed their goals. Plus, I'll be sharing 10 Success Secrets that you can apply today and over time to achieve all your dreams.

What you see in me now as a leader and multiple 6-figure business owner wasn't always so. I was once in that very same spot you are now. I had to adopt a mindset of growth and evolution while prioritizing myself so that I could step into my power, get out of my own way, break through the glass ceiling, and move forward beyond it.

Too often, my impatience, fear, and doubt would take over, and I could feel myself in those moments slipping back into the emotional abyss of feeling not good enough. Through hard work, determined focus, and consistent self-care, I was able to work past my own hurdles, embrace my true power, and unlock the key to 6-figure success. It's my pleasure to share that with you now.

The first step and overarching concept is to adopt a mindset of relentless growth and evolution. Ask yourself: What can I learn today that will move me closer to achieving 6-figure success? It may be something small or big that you discover, but allow yourself to be open to learning new things every day, if even for just 15 minutes. This can include reading books, researching online, taking classes, courses, coaching programs related to your business, or simply watching inspiring videos that can give you the fuel and motivation to keep going.

The second step is to prioritize yourself. This means taking time out of each day, even for as little as 15 minutes, to practice self-care practices such as meditating, journaling, yoga or stretching, walking in nature, etc. It may also mean investing in yourself with courses or coaching programs that will help you accelerate your progress towards achieving 6-figure success faster than you could on your own.

Finally, create an action plan, and be sure to track your progress so that you can see the results clearly unfolding before you! Celebrate each milestone, and don't forget to reward yourself along the way. Deal?

The 3-Part System, along with the 10 Success Secrets, is designed to help you:

- Adopt a mindset of relentless growth and evolution.
- Prioritize yourself as you rise up through your 6-figure success journey.

This system provides simple yet powerful steps that will help you maximize your potential and create the life of abundance and fulfillment that you desire. It's time to take control of your destiny. Let's get started on building the foundation!

Your Success Formula:

$$IV + CPR + SOS$$

Phase 1: Gain Crystal Clarity

IV = Identify IT! Visualize IT!

The first phase in this system is *Identify IT! Visualize IT!* This phase challenges you to identify and visualize what it will look like when you achieve your 6-figure success goal. You must answer the following at this stage through research and self-reflection:

- What kind of businesses, lifestyle, or projects will you be able to pursue?
- Who are the people that will support you on this journey?
- How do you want to feel in terms of confidence, security, and joy?

When these questions have been answered, and clear visualizations have been created, go ahead and move into phase 2 to take actionable steps toward your dreams!

Phase 2: Develop Laser Focus

CPR = Create IT! Practice IT! Ritualize IT!

The second phase of the system encourages you to *Create IT! Practice IT! Ritualize IT!* Here, it is essential that you take advantage of the tools and techniques at your disposal to bring your dreams to fruition. This includes developing effective systems and routines, engaging in meaningful self-care practices, taking actionable steps toward business success, such as marketing and selling, and building a strong support network. Implementing these practices into your life and business will help you stay motivated as you strive toward 6-figure success.

In this phase, first, create a plan. Once you have your plan, put it into practice. Lastly, ritualize your practice; remember, success comes from consistency over time. Creating a plan helps give you focus and clarity on what needs to get done in order to reach your goal.

Putting your plan into practice allows you to make sure that every step taken is an effective one. As well it gives you the opportunity to fine-tune any areas where improvement can be made. Ritualizing these practices through regular repetition and dedication, you will be able to stay motivated and committed on your journey toward 6-figure success. All these steps are essential in building a strong foundation for achieving this level of excellence.

Phase 3: Create Meaningful Boundaries

S.O.S. = Structure, Systems, and Scheduling OVER Stress!

The final phase in this system encourages you to create a *Slip Up Plan*. This is an important step, as it helps to ensure that no matter what challenge or obstacle arises, you'll have a plan for recovery and success. It's easy to get discouraged if we make one mistake after another. Your *Slip Up Plan* should include ways to minimize mistakes and how to bounce back quickly from any missteps taken along the way. This may include making sure that you start each day with clear intentions and goals, scheduling regular check-ins with yourself on progress made towards your 6-figure success, and getting an accountability partner or a coach who can provide timely encouragement when needed. By having a comprehensive *Slip Up Plan* in place, you will be able to stay focused and on track.

Creating a *Slip Up Plan* consists of *Structure, Systems,* and *Scheduling to avoid Stress.* It's easy to get overwhelmed with all the tasks and responsibilities associated with achieving 6-figure success. To keep from getting bogged down by stress, it's important that you create a structure that will help you stay organized while also allowing room for flexibility. This may include maintaining a productive daily schedule, developing systems for tracking progress made toward goals, and utilizing helpful tools like task lists and calendar reminders. By following these simple steps, you can ensure that your journey toward 6-figure success is as enjoyable and rewarding as possible!

By using this 3-Part System, you'll gain crystal clarity, develop laser focus, and create meaningful boundaries so that you can be on your way to 6-figure success in no time!

Next, I'll show you 10 powerful success secrets that will help unleash your full potential and maximize your opportunities. From establishing a strong foundation of personal development to mastering effective communication techniques, these success secrets are designed to set you up for lasting success in everything you do.

10 of the most important success secrets to keep in mind to remain calm, clear, and focused:

Secret #1: Set Big Goals and Take Massive Action

Setting big goals is a critical part of achieving success. You need to have a clear target to aim for, and then take massive action to reach it. This involves developing a plan and putting in the hard work necessary to achieve your goals.

Stay focused, and don't let yourself be discouraged.

Secret #2: Develop a Strong Work Ethic and Focus on Becoming the Best at What You Do

This involves putting in the hard work necessary to reach your goals, consistently. If creating a 6-figure business were easy, everyone would do it. That is exactly why it's also important to maintain a positive attitude and keep forging your way forward. Developing a strong work ethic involves:

$$C + T + E$$

$$=$$

Commitment + Time + Effort

Commit to your goals, take the necessary time, and make the effort to achieve them. Embrace personal growth and self-development. Constantly seek out new opportunities to learn and grow as a person. Learning never stops; stay hungry for knowledge, push yourself beyond your comfort zone, and challenge yourself to become better every day.

Surround yourself with other successful people who can inspire you and point you in the right direction. One of the most powerful success secrets is surrounding yourself with people who have achieved what you are striving for. These people can provide invaluable advice, motivation, and support on your journey.

Secret #3: Constantly Improve Your Skills and Knowledge for Growth as an Entrepreneur

In order to constantly improve your skills and knowledge for growth as an entrepreneur, you'll need to be constantly learning new strategies and techniques. This involves reading books, attending seminars, and participating in online courses. It's also important to practice what you learn so that you can apply it to your business.

Note: *Although you want to always be learning, do not allow yourself to stay stuck comfortably gaining knowledge and not using it.*

Create a clear vision and establish goals for yourself. To do this, you need to take some time to sit down and think about your ideal future - What kind of life would you like to lead after achieving success? Once you have established that vision, create specific, achievable goals for yourself. Break these goals down into smaller chunks so that they are more manageable, and seek out those who can help you get where you want to go.

Secret #4: Believe in Yourself and Your Ability to Succeed No Matter What Others Say

This involves having a positive attitude and staying focused on your goals. No matter what obstacles or challenges you may face, don't let yourself get discouraged; keep pushing forward until you achieve your dreams. Stay focused, and don't let yourself be influenced by others; believe in yourself and your ability to succeed, and you will reach your goals. Belief in yourself is essential to your success.

You must have an inner belief that you are capable of reaching any goal that you set out for yourself, as well as have a willingness to take risks and put in the necessary effort to achieve it. Remind yourself daily of your capabilities and focus on the things that will bring you closer to success. Don't let others' negative opinions or fears stop you from believing in what's possible for you. Be confident in your decisions, and keep pushing forward!

1. **Don't give up at the first sign of adversity. No one said that achieving 6-figure success would be easy, and the journey may present you with many challenges.** It's important to remain motivated and focused on your goals, even when things get tough. Don't give up at

the first sign of adversity. Instead, take a step back and remind yourself why you started this journey in the first place. Evaluate what went wrong and figure out how you can improve upon it going forward. Any successful entrepreneur will tell you that their projects went through many rough patches before they eventually achieved success - so don't let any setbacks define your future! With hard work, dedication, and the right attitude, anything is possible if you stay motivated and keep pushing forward. Believe in yourself and never give up on your dreams - you won't regret it. Remember, anything is possible if you keep believing in yourself and never give up on your dreams. You can do it!

2. **Take risks and put yourself out there, even if you're afraid of failure.** Taking risks is an essential part of achieving success as an entrepreneur. Although it can be scary to put yourself out there and take chances, this is

necessary for growth and progress. You must be willing to step outside of your comfort zone and try new things to find what works best for you. There is no one quite like you, and you will find your own style in entrepreneurship. When taking risks, it's important to assess the potential outcome beforehand so that you have some idea of the results that you could expect. Don't let fear of failure prevent you from making decisions - if something doesn't work out, there are always valuable lessons to learn from it. Remember that failure is not a sign of defeat; instead, it should be seen as a learning opportunity on your journey to success. Take risks and put yourself out there, and you won't regret it! Success is a journey; don't expect to achieve everything overnight.

3. **Embrace change and be willing to adapt as needed.** Successful entrepreneurs know that they need to be flexible and embrace change in

order to stay ahead of the game. Being agile is key; staying open-minded and learning from new experiences will help you grow and take your business to a whole new level. Don't be afraid to experiment with different strategies or processes, as it's often these small changes that can make the biggest difference in your success. Also, don't assume that something will always work the same way - be willing to think outside the box and try different approaches if needed. Embracing change allows us to adjust our plans based on what works best for us so we can continue making progress toward our goals without feeling stuck or overwhelmed by a rigid system. Keep your eye on the prize, and stay focused on your goals in a firm yet flexible manner.

4. **<u>Be patient, and don't give up on your dreams or goals, no matter how long it takes.</u>** Successful entrepreneurs understand that reaching the top is a marathon, not a

sprint. It can take years of hard work and dedication to achieve the level of success that you desire. Don't be discouraged if progress happens slowly – focus on small wins along the way and stay consistent in your efforts. Celebrate each milestone as proof that you are moving closer to achieving success. Be patient with yourself throughout this journey; Rome wasn't built in a day! Don't forget why you started this journey in the first place, and remember that with hard work, perseverance, and patience, anything is possible. The journey to 6-figures might take time, but the results will be worth it as long as you approach it with intention and awareness while embracing these success habits.

5. **Identify and prioritize your core values.** When building a successful business, these values are the foundation for everything you do and will help you stay focused on what matters most. They also have the power to

keep you motivated during difficult times and provide guidance when making tough decisions. Identifying core values can be an empowering experience that allows you to align your actions with those of others who share similar beliefs, creating a powerful network that can lead to greater success. Additionally, when others know what's important to you, they will be more likely to want to work with or invest in your business. Knowing your core values will help ensure that you build a 6-figure + business that reflects who you are as a person. Never lose sight of who you are.

6. **Self-care and success habits as a 6-figure entrepreneur and beyond.** As a 6-figure entrepreneur, it is essential to have a healthy balance between work and self-care. Self-care habits such as exercising regularly, eating nourishing food, getting enough sleep, and engaging in activities that bring joy are

essential for maintaining physical and mental well-being. These habits will help you stay focused and energized so that you can put your best foot forward on the path to success. Additionally, developing routines that focus on relaxation and mindfulness can help reduce stress levels and improve productivity. Taking time each day to practice self-care can make all the difference when it comes to achieving your goals. Investing in yourself is just as important as investing in your business; after all, if you don't take care of yourself, you won't be able to succeed. With the right habits and self-care practices, you can become a 6-figure+ entrepreneur with ease and stay successful for years to come.

Ultimately, becoming a successful 6-figure+ entrepreneur isn't easy. The real secret is that it takes hard work, dedication, and patience to reach the level of success you desire. However, by setting realistic goals, recognizing and prioritizing your core values, developing effective habits and routines, and investing in self-care practices, you can turn your dreams into reality.

Always remember that even small changes can make the biggest difference in your success – never underestimate yourself or give up on your dreams! With these habits as part of your daily routine, there's no limit to what you can achieve.

Allison Barnett

There comes a day when you decide you are worth more. That you deserve more. That you are meant for more. And when that day comes, you will receive it.

~ Allison Barnett

They say that the road to hell is paved with good intentions. The same could be said for the path to a 6-figure salary. It's a journey that many of us walk, yet it can often feel like we are traveling uphill, in the snow, without shoes.

Want to add more zeros to your paycheck? No problem! Just dive off the cliff, bang your head against the wall a few times, admit that sleep is overrated, and sing the alphabet backward. If you are still standing after this, we can begin to discuss adding a zero or two to your income and bank account. If this sounds familiar, then you have probably ridden life's financial roller coaster. You've probably fallen off a few times, too. Yet, you are still determined to get the win and walk that yellow brick road to financial freedom. Am I right? If you are reading this, the answer is probably yes.

So, let me introduce myself, because we have a lot to talk about. I'm Allison Barnett, a lifelong entrepreneur, intuitive Realtor, multi-6-figure earner, and money healer who has been through hell and back a few times on my money journey. I earned the scars and the t-shirt, and I wouldn't have it any other way. This path allowed me to crack the code, and now I help others to do the same.

Money. Oh, how I love money. It's comical how uncomfortable people are when it becomes the topic of discussion. The word alone causes so much drama and emotion! For some, it is an addiction. For others, it is the root of all evil. For me, it's the feeling of a true love affair. The bane of my existence. My biggest desire. The worst relationship I ever had. The means to the freedom that I truly craved. It seemed like there was never enough money in my world, yet there was always enough money to survive.

I'm pretty sure my relationship with money began way before I was born. We must have been soulmates or star-crossed lovers, depending on the perspective. Meeting up, and then passing in the night. Then, waiting for the next time we could be together, followed by the joy of that fleeting moment and then the sorrow of it passing. Honestly, you could probably write a really great romance novel with money as one of the characters. But I wanted more than this cycle of lust and loss. I wanted money to stay forever… As you can tell, I'm a dreamer.

I've always had big dreams that never could quite fit in with the life I was living. It was laughable, considering most people believed that my family was rich. We were rich – just not financially. I grew up in a typical middle-class family with the house, the car, and the three kids. My parents never let us feel the crunch, and they were very creative in making sure we had what we needed. My bike was used, but had really cool red wheels. We went out to eat, but there was always a request to honor the extra coupon. Birthday parties were usually at home, where my mom dared to host a bunch of kids for cake and art projects. My sister and I shared a room.

Somehow, it all worked – though, admittedly, I still have the memories of the battlecruiser car that no one wanted to be seen in and the designer-ish labels that were sewn onto our jeans for the extra cool look. When I wanted something that my parents refused to pay for, I always found a way to get it. From birthday gift requests and grandparent bribes to my own stellar selling skills, I was made for 'when there's a will, there's a way.'

Trust me, there was always a way. In fact, I was probably around five or six when I decided to sell my drawings to the neighbors. I thought it was brilliant, but apparently, my mom disagreed. She made me return the money, unimpressed by my entrepreneurial skills. Some serious ugly crying was involved, yet a star was born, full of sass, determination, and dreams. I adopted the mindset that work equals pay. Period. The more I work, the more I make, the more I can have. So, I babysat, sold greeting cards door to door, sold candy bars at school, worked my way through college and law school, grew up, and worked some more.

What seemed to slip my awareness was the constant need for more, just to keep up with all that I wanted once I had my own overhead. Suddenly, I was living a money in, money out lifestyle, with maxed-out credit cards and rarely enough money left over to do the things I really wanted and dreamed of. The cliché of two steps forward, ten steps back was real. You know that feeling, right? A constant need to work to make more money that disappears faster than it comes in. It's an evil cycle that I couldn't seem to stop, and I wanted off of the ride.

If I could just make 6-figures!! I finished law school, married the love of my life, and started waiting tables for extra money. I made the decision not to practice law, deciding to focus on real estate instead. While I knew it would take time to grow, I was absolutely certain that I would make all the zeros and more. I had student loans to pay off and big plans for travel, babies, a house, and a boat.

The man I married also had big dreams of owning his own business. In my head, we were the ultimate power couple destined to live our best lives. It was inevitable, right??! We just needed the money to do so. And we got it! I chose to work for a builder in a housing boom and made the first 6-figures that would launch us to the luxury life we wanted. It was phenomenal!

Kind of. Unfortunately, that 6-figure year came at a huge cost. I never saw my husband because we both worked all the time. I missed out on the parties, the weddings, the travel…because I couldn't take a day off! At the same time, my husband developed this mysterious illness that no one could figure out, and I was willing to spend all that we had and could borrow to heal him. Credit card payments were increasing by double and triple, and the truth was, I was broke. I was making 6-figures, wondering what I was doing wrong.

So, I worked some more. If there was ever a queen of the side hustle, it was me. I sold cookware, wraps, makeup, home décor….The list was endless, and there was always a way to make the extra cash that we needed. My friends seemed to thrive and take amazing vacations, yet here I was, feeling broke and embarrassed because I couldn't seem to ever get ahead. We looked like we made a lot of money. We paid taxes like we did, too! However, net income minus car repairs, private health insurance, self-employment taxes, and groceries equaled serious disappointment and negative bank balances. The cycle continued for years, earning well, yet living paycheck to paycheck.

It all came to a screeching halt with the housing crash of 2008. The builder I worked for went bankrupt and disappeared, along with the twelve thousand dollars they owed me. Let me repeat that – my commission of TWELVE THOUSAND DOLLARS disappeared in an instant. I was unemployed, in a field where there were no jobs available and plenty of bills coming in that required the money I was no longer receiving. Fortunately, my husband's business stayed afloat just enough to keep us going. But it was a time of uncomfortable decisions, like which bills to no longer pay while we tried to stabilize. Money and I were no longer friends, but God and

I became bosom buddies as I prayed for guidance and help every second of the day.

In the darkness, there is light. And by light, I mean light seekers and light workers, also known as psychics, healers, and energy workers. The world of energetics and limitless abundance. I was obsessively exploring the spiritual world because the human world stopped making sense. I did all the things I was supposed to. I followed the rules and was kind to my neighbors and animals. I deserved magic and miracles, but my life was in a state of ruins that only divine intervention could get back on track.

I always wanted to be a psychic, and with way too much time on my hands, I binged on my favorite episodes of Sylvia Brown and other famous intuitives. Even better, I had a friend with 'the gift.' We would go to lunch, where she kindly paid, read cards for me, and gave me hope when needed. So what if we had to sit by the window so I could keep an eye on my car to make sure it wasn't repossessed? She fed my soul and introduced me to other light workers. She taught me to read my own tarot and encouraged my channeling abilities. Our time together opened a world full of possibilities that I was grateful for.

Even when the bills were late, the car was repossessed, and we were fighting to keep our home. I was sure that money hated me, but I knew that there had to be a way for my 6-figure income to return quickly. Maybe I could win the lottery? That was my favorite answer. Forget 6-figures. I want seven. Or eight! How many zeros can you fit on a check because there will never be enough zeros in my bank account.

Wealth is like a computer program where we need a bunch of zeros after every primary digit. Add five or more zeros to achieve the pillar post of success. The first level is the coveted 6-figures. If you think about it, society has placed the 6-figure income on a pedestal. We have this grand illusion that money is hard to make and that there isn't enough for everyone to enjoy. But what if society is wrong about this rare, precious commodity? What if money is plentiful and readily available whenever we want it? In the world of energetics and light workers, money is energy. It is a beautiful vibration that comes and goes the more you play with it. You can choose to receive money, or you can block it so it stays away. The more you spend, the more you will have returned to you. The more you make, the more you can help yourself and others. Money is love. It's a source of freedom. It's a reason to celebrate. And it is normal to ask for more. The abundance mentality is mind-blowing when you've been taught to hustle and trade dollars for hours. It's like the weight of the world lifts off of your shoulders, and you have been handed the keys to a magical land where you just have to believe to receive.

For a girl who couldn't seem to find the roadmap to a better life, this utopia was a dream come true! I began to forge my path to financial freedom. I spent years changing my mindset, rewriting my story, and learning to play with money. I expanded my gifts, manifesting easily and amplifying my ability to earn and receive. I decided that the constant hustle wasn't working for me. I let go of the frustration, the pain, the disgust, and the shame. I recognized that I was worthy of more and deserved to have all my dreams come true. It took some time, but I managed to wrap my head around the idea that money was mine whenever I wanted it – and I liked it that way.

While I was growing in the spiritual realm, I also found a job that, once again, proved I was never meant to be an employee. So, like all millionaires in the making, I diversified. I launched my own wine jelly company and returned to real estate. I took on side projects when they were offered. I was open to any idea and opportunity that came my way. It was still a time of living paycheck to paycheck, but I could see the light at the end of the tunnel and was determined to get there.

We took a few hits financially over the years. Another boss decided not to pay me a 5-figure commission. Life happened, with more car repairs and business expenses pouring in. But I held true to my vision and created a game out of making more money. Affirmations and journaling became a daily ritual. I made friends with money, always expressing gratitude for what I had and how the money helped to provide it. I was thankful for the roof over my head that I fought hard to keep. I embraced a gratefulness for all things money, including the empty bank account that just paid all of my bills.

It was exciting to watch as money flowed in faster. My manifesting abilities were on high, and I knew I had all the tools to make magic happen.

The love affair with money was officially back in full swing, and the doors to the 6-figure income were reopening. It was amazing! Now, I realize this sounds like a fairy tale, but if life imitates art, this will all make sense and probably make you more money too.

Imagine Jerry McGuire screaming, 'Show me the money!!' and instantly, Mary Poppins walks in with her spoon full of sugar and magical purse, handing over huge chunks of money in what appears to be an unlimited supply. Jerry expresses gratitude. Mary smiles and says she will see him again soon. And this scenario plays on repeat, just like the movie, Groundhog Day.

THIS can really happen. In fact, I know many people living this exact life. As far-fetched as it seems, this is a real-life scenario when you remove the movie titles and characters. This could be your life. I can honestly say it's happening in mine, and as you know, that wasn't always the case. I had more woes than money and thought I was being punished for something I did in a past life. It was depressing, embarrassing, and heartbreaking to the point that I finally had enough, flipped the switch, changed my attitude, and started seeing magic happen. I bought into the fairy tale. Did it happen that fast? No. I had to retrain my money habits while rewriting my money story. I started making friends with more money and better stories than the one above. I joined coaching programs that taught me more about energy, frequency, magic, and abundance. I expanded my faith in God and myself. I celebrated more and complained less. I let go of the past and embraced the future. And I learned that it was actually easier for me to make thousands than it was to find a single penny, even though I celebrate both.

Admittedly, money started flowing faster, but it still wasn't sticking around. I was steadily getting closer to that 6-figure life again, finally breathing easily when Covid hit and the world shut down. It wasn't pretty. This time, it was my husband's business that came to a halt. Our income tanked. The fun discussions about which bills should and shouldn't get paid were starting to happen, and I wondered if all of my efforts were in vain. Two steps forward, ten steps back.

And all I could think was, F--- that!! It was the middle of the night when I woke up with a very clear mind and firm decision that there was no way in hell that I was returning to the money rollercoaster. It was a huge no for me. Not an option. I immediately started journaling to channel guidance. I did some middle-of-the-night manifesting. I activated a very clear intention that money was flowing in regardless of the economy. I channeled some extra encouragement from the angels and anchored myself in my mindset and a 6-figure income. I would receive it with ease.

And so I did. A big shift in energy was needed, so I sold off my jelly business and expanded my real estate business with a brokerage that added even more income streams. It was just what I needed. Clients appeared out of thin air. There was a steady flow of real estate closings, and even in the competitive market, all of my clients bought and sold their homes easily. I made myself available to coach more realtors and business owners to higher levels of success, too. I discovered I was a money healer and block buster for many, easily seeing through the chaos, clearing the path, and helping my clients manifest more. I started to pay my bills months in advance, which was a miracle.

I made 6-figures easily that year and far more than that ever since. It was that single moment and firm decision that cleared the path and allowed money to flow again. It was the best decision I ever made.

Life is a journey, and finances can be a rollercoaster. I am truly grateful for the lessons I learned and the gifts I received on my path to 6-figure success. When I opened the spiritual door to the limitless world that we live in, I didn't expect to receive the gifts of channeling and manifesting. I didn't know that I would become a money healer, business coach, and multi-6-figure earner.

But the journey is full of magical twists and turns. You just have to know what you want and believe enough to receive it. You never know... you might just find yourself with even more than you dreamed.

Sherice Kral

The Ultimate Success Formula

Humans are incredible creatures. We can lose everything, get our lives ripped apart, and lose our future and purpose. Yet somehow, in just a few years, we can build a new home or family, get back everything plus more than we had before, create new goals, and have a more exciting future!

We can take anything, including death, and reproduce new growth from it. Humans grow. It's what we're best at! We grow plants, products, futures, and even other Humans. Sometimes, I think we forget how uniquely natural and strong our ability to grow is.

If you're reading this, you're likely the kind of person who has what it takes to build a successful business. You've probably heard that it takes a certain kind of person to be a successful entrepreneur, and that's true to a certain extent.

But the truth is, if you have the natural ability to grow a business, you can take it to whatever revenue level you'd like. All you need are three key pillars to get you there.

There are three key pillars to success in business:

1. Business owner's psychology.
2. Strategy that works.
3. Influence to guide others and build communities.

If you have the right mindset, the right strategy, and the ability to influence others, you can take your business to the top.

Some might say I got lucky when I first started out. I was working for two leadership coaches who made over 3.4 million each month, and they taught me to build a 7-figure coaching business myself. I'm nowhere near their revenue, but making that first million felt like I'd finally "made it." I could take a breath and relax. This is what I like to call The WaveBreak. The moment when you finally realize you've made it. Everyone will reach this moment at a different point because we all view success differently.

The most important lesson I learned from my first mentors was that success in business was 80% psychology and only 20% skill. Today, everyone just wants the strategies (and I can create some bad-ass strategies!), but so many entrepreneurs or hobbyists turn their noses up at anything that reminds them of mindset work. Not surprisingly, the people who get stuck in this belief ultimately fail.

As we go through each of these three pillars today, I encourage you to trust the process. There's a reason that two of these focus on your mindset, and only one focuses on actionable strategy. That being said, I will offer you a unique strategy that can give you a jumpstart in any phase of your business if you've plateaued or are just starting out.

Business Owner's Psychology

If you want to be successful in business, you need to have the right mindset. You need to be confident and believe in yourself and your product or service. You need to be willing to take risks, and you need to be resilient in the face of setbacks. You need to have a positive outlook and be solutions-oriented. If you can master your own psychology, you'll be well on your way to success.

One lesson that so many new entrepreneurs and established but plateaued entrepreneurs have is:

• Not building an emotional business.

When we build emotionally, we often trip ourselves up because we cling to plans, strategies, looks, and beliefs about our business, even if they hurt our ability to grow.

For example, a popular emotional belief is that we will lose our clients and never get new ones if we raise our prices. It becomes a belief based on an unknown fear without any research to back it up.

Every time I've walked clients or an audience member through raising their prices by 30% using research and logic, they soon find that raising their prices was an incredible next step in their business.

Fear is the number one driver of our lack of action. In fact, psychology states that every time we fail to take action, it's to avoid pain (fear is the most common type of pain). So, in the example above, the fear or pain that their businesses may crumble was more important than the desire for pleasure that raising prices and getting more money would give them.

To avoid getting sucked into emotional stuck points as you grow your business, ask yourself these questions below every time you can't get yourself to take action or make a change:

1. Is that belief really true? – How do you know it's true...what's the proof?

2. What is driving me right now: Pleasure or pain?

3. What am I trying to avoid or run toward with this belief or action?

4. Does this help or hurt my business?

Taking these questions seriously is a good start to coaching yourself through a stuck point.

Strategy that Works

No matter how great your product or service is, it won't get you very far if you don't have a solid business strategy. You need to know who your target market is, what needs your product or service meets, and how you will reach your target market. You need to set goals, track your progress, and be constantly tweaking and evolving your strategy to ensure it's as effective as possible.

This is where an experienced business consultant or coach comes in handy. Having an expert help you build strategies allows you to grow faster and with less pain. I strongly believe that coaches and consultants need experience before they can successfully work with people. The only exception is if someone gets trained and certified in a specific method and only uses that method in their work (until they gain their own experience). With business coaching or consulting, it's more crucial to have experience because there are simply too many changes in business development. Personally, I suggest only working with someone who's built a $1 million revenue or more business themselves before in a coaching or consulting business. Six-figure businesses are still considered "new" or baby businesses in the coaching and consulting world.

While in another industry, these are expert-level businesses, and you need to have the experience of building 7-figures before I would consider you a good candidate for helping others build a business.

So, do your research when looking for someone to take your business to the next level!

- Start Selling Without an Audience –

You've Likely Heard That You Need An Audience To Sell To.

And While That's True To Some Extent, You Can Totally Sell Without One! Below is a simple 4-step strategy outline to do this. You can also use this strategy to build awareness and jumpstart more growth if your established business has plateaued.

1. Know what you're selling

If you don't have this one clearly laid out, the next steps won't help you at all...It may even hurt your future progress. So don't skip this step.

If you don't know what you're selling but you know what industry/niche you're in, ask yourself these questions:

❧ What is a big Need and Want that your industry has?

(Just because people need something, doesn't mean they want it.)

❧ How do they want this Need to be fulfilled?

❧ Can you pre-sell or build this with the help of a couple of ideal clients?

❧ Can you create a couple of photo ads on Canva to use as promotion and a landing page to purchase?

2. Build a list of experts you know who have an ideal client audience for you.

DO NOT put experts on this list if they have corporate CEO's and you want to sell to stay-at-home mom-preneurs.

Make sure these experts have your ideal clientele.

Then:

- If you're close friends, ask them to bring you in as a guest speaker into their Facebook group Live, podcast, blog, or YouTube channel.

- If you don't have any relationship with these people, start building one! Comment daily on their posts, learn from them, tell them how they've helped you grow, and consistently promote them to people you know.

- Ask your friends, family, and network if they know someone who's looking for guest speakers inside of their audience.

- Start networking; join groups, attend live events (virtual and in-person), and broaden your network to find more experts.

3. Schedule guest teaching sessions.

Now that you have a list, reach out to each person on it and ask if they would get value from bringing you in! (If they don't trust your expertise, this won't work. So send them some videos of you teaching in your element, or audio of you talking about your zone of wisdom.)

- Schedule at least 1 per week for two months. Preferably 2 per week! That's 8-16 guest events.

- Make sure to CLEARLY promote one action at the end of each event: "Go to my link [xyz] to sign up for [offer title]!"

4. (Most often missed!) Reach out to the host for a testimonial.

If someone got all of the steps up until now, I rarely see them do this. Get those dang testimonials!

Personally, I love using VideoAsk. They can offer you a video, audio, or written review with a click of a button.

This simple, yet super secret squirrel strategy is the BEST strategy to use when first starting out as an entrepreneur. Or if you're going to launch a new offer.

Lastly, what's the best thing to sell at the end of your guest appearances? ...Since you don't have an audience yet, I highly suggest selling your newsletter subscription. It's not a monetary sale, so you won't be making money. But your email list is the golden river that runs through your business...So get to building that ASAP!

Influencing Others: To Guide People and Build Communities

If you want to be above average in any business or career, you need to be able to influence others.

You need to be able to build relationships and networks, inspire others to believe in your product or service, as well as lead and motivate a team (or your clients). If you can learn to influence others, you'll open the doors of opportunity.

Leadership is influence. Nothing more, nothing less.

A mother influencing her children to become better people is leadership.

An employee who truly cares for their team members both above and below them, watches out for them, encourages them to reach for new opportunities, and protects them, is leadership.

A teacher who truly cares if their students learn their lessons each day and grow themselves, is considered leadership.

We often have a negative taste in our mouths about the word "leadership" because, until recently, it's been a term coined by big corporate, old, white CEO's. In reality, most of them practice authoritarianism and manipulation, not leadership.

To try and break away from those self-centered CEO's, people started creating different types of leadership, such as servant leadership, or transactional leadership. They aren't wrong. But at the simplest level, there is Influence, then manipulation and force. There is leadership, and there is being a boss.

That's the beauty of language; everything can mean something different within a variety of contexts. So, don't get caught up on the words I use here. Because it just doesn't matter at the end of the day.

The key lesson with influence is that:

1. There is no such thing as Luck in life. Only the level of influence you've built brings you opportunities.

2. You must build influence and start at the beginning with each person. If you're a new boss, focus on building influence with each individual person underneath you. As an entrepreneur, build influence with each client, each partner, each independent contractor you hire, and each employee.

3. Anytime you want to tell someone what to do or guide them, you need influence. This includes client sessions, sales, rate negotiations, and more.

My goal here today wasn't to tell you all about myself. It was to give you the most valuable information that, alone, could build you a 6-figure business if this book is the only thing you have to get you there. Keep learning, continue growing, and never give up on your dreams. Just learn to adjust the vehicle that gets you there.

Tony Babcock

Welcome to my world, boo, where I'll share with you my journey and the valuable insights that I've learned along the way that have helped me unlock unlimited wealth and success as a 6-figure business coach (and also led me to realize that this wealth and success doesn't really matter as much as I thought it did). Also, full disclosure - I am listening to Broadway musical soundtracks right now as I write this. I am THAT bitch!

My name is Tony Babcock, and I'm a motivational speaker, NLP Practitioner, certified life coach, an award-winning filmmaker/actor (thus the Broadway), and a BIG KID. But let me tell you, I haven't always been this successful, confident, or honest about my music tastes.

Growing up, I was an awkward, closeted gay teen desperately trying to prove myself and struggling to find my place in the world. I was bullied (mostly by myself), and my self-esteem was non-existent. It wasn't until I was forced to discover the power of just *being myself* that I began to turn my life around. This was further explored when I learned about two powerful practices: NLP and improv.

I'm assuming you know what improv is (fun fact: I recently starred in a film with Colin Mochrie from *Whose Line is It Anyway* - I can die happy now), but I should explain what NLP is. NLP stands for neuro-linguistic programming, a technique that uses language and behavior to change a person's thoughts and actions. It's a powerful tool that I use in my coaching practices to help my clients achieve their goals and overcome their limiting beliefs.

Okay, back to the story - let me be real with you. My journey to becoming a successful 6-figure business coach wasn't all rainbows and butterflies. I've had my fair share of setbacks, failures, and challenges along the way. But, I've learned (often painfully) that it's these experiences that have shaped me into the person I am today, and have given me the wisdom, knowledge, and calling to help others.

So, let's get to some of the secrets I've picked up along the way. After all, that's why you're here, right?

One of the most important secrets I've learned along the way is that you can't have consistent results without the *3 P's:* Purpose, Passion, and Perseverance. When I started my coaching practice, I knew that I wanted to help people achieve their goals and live their best lives. I knew I had a real message to impart to others and the life experience to back it up. I knew all this, yet my business was getting NOWHERE. And I mean NOWHERE. My first coaching business was an acting studio, and I remember my first year, I made a whopping $5000! Don't get me wrong, how amazing it was that I created income out of ideas in my head - but at about

$400 per month, I certainly wasn't putting food on the table. And you know what? I didn't care because I was doing what I loved and helping people succeed. And that's why PASSION is a key ingredient! I was passionate about what I was doing, and it gave me the motivation to keep going, even when things got tough.

But passion alone isn't enough. You also need to have a clear sense of purpose. What is it that you want to achieve? What impact do you want to leave on this world? Without a clear sense of purpose, your passion can fizzle out quickly - and this is exactly what was happening to me because I didn't have a clear, specific mission. With my clients today, I call it your *Soul Mission.* That one thing you are on this planet to do - that relates to movement - in one way, it's a goal, but it's so much bigger than a goal. It's a legacy. Without this, you will fall into that state where you feel so directionless, stagnant, and almost like you're living underneath your potential. Have you been there? Are you there now? Every self-employed person on the planet feels this from time to time - so don't worry, if you are feeling this now, you are perfectly normal.

That's why I always encourage my clients to dig deep and identify their purpose. It's not always an easy process, but it's essential if you want to achieve success and fulfillment.

Still, passion AND purpose are not going to lead to ongoing success. You need the third ingredient: *Perseverance,* or everything will fall apart. Perseverance is about resiliently continuing when shit gets tough (and trust me, it will). Perseverance is the athlete-level commitment to your success and mission. Your Passion and Purpose fuel it, but it is the ongoing ACTION you take despite a ton of fear. Take a moment right now and figure out your PASSION, PURPOSE, and PERSEVERANCE levels on a scale from 1 (low) to 10 (stratosphere).

This is called gap-mapping. Now you know where the work is…

Another valuable secret I've learned is the mindset-hacking. Your mindset plays a crucial role in your success. And it's the number one thing that derails you when things are too hard (or too easy). If you have a shitty mindset, you'll always find reasons why you can't achieve your goals. But, if you can hack into that mindset, you'll see opportunities everywhere and be more likely to take action.

One of my favorite ways to hack into my shitty thinking is something I learned in acting classes in NYC and that we all learned on the playground. It's super simple. Jumping Jacks. When you feel undesirable emotions due to a governing negative thought/belief system, instead of wallowing in it, force yourself to do 25 jumping jacks. By the time you are done, you will have moved from your overthinking mind, to your ever-present body, and worked through 90%

of the emotion you're struggling with so you can actually face what is really bothering you. Now, you are set up for the next step.

I'm a big believer in the power of affirmations and visualization. Affirmations are positive statements that you repeat to yourself to reinforce positive beliefs and behaviors. Visualization is the process of imagining yourself achieving your goals and visualizing the steps you need to take to get there.

These techniques may seem simple, but they're incredibly powerful. They've helped me and my clients overcome limiting beliefs, boost our confidence, and achieve our goals. Once you have *jumping-jack'd* into your body, employ one or both of these strategies.

One of the biggest challenges I see in my coaching practice is the fear of failure. It's natural to feel scared when stepping out of your comfort zone and pursuing your dreams (what I call the danger zone), but it's important not to let that fear hold you back from your soul mission. As Lisa Nichols says: *Do it Scared.* One of the most important things I teach my clients is the importance of reframing their mindset around failure. Rather than seeing failure as a negative thing, I encourage my clients to see it as a learning opportunity by *Friending Failure.* By reframing their perspective this way, my clients can approach challenges with more confidence and resilience and a "Is this really a big deal?" *attitude.* Additionally, they are better equipped to bounce back from setbacks and keep moving forward toward their goals.

I've learned that failure is not the opposite of success, but rather a really integral part of the journey. Remember that acting studio I was running? Well, cut to years later, and there I was, lying down on the studio floor, an emotional mess. Feeling the weight of 200K of debt, little to no business, and a FOR SALE sign in the window, I was a mess. Little did I know then, this was a huge defining moment in my life. A pivotal one. I felt myself going over the edge of pain into a place of humor. Yes, you read that right. When I realized that Failure was just a tricky bitch trying to teach me something, I realized I could actually make friends with it and even thank it. This was the moment when I realized my mission, passion, and purpose were bigger than any studio - any one experience - and that my ability to *find a new way* was my best asset.

Every successful person has experienced deep failure at some point in their lives, but what sets them apart is their ability to learn from those failures and keep going.

If I hadn't listened to that inner knowing, I have no idea where I would be today. I certainly wouldn't be running four successful businesses, living with my dream partner, and writing this chapter.

So, here's another secret. I always encourage my clients to adopt an *Is It Possible* mindset. An '*IIP*' mindset is the belief that your abilities and intelligence can be developed through hard work, dedication, and perseverance. With this mindset, you see failures as opportunities to learn and grow, rather than as a reflection of your abilities. With every challenging situation, you are asking the question: *Is it possible..?* For example, *is it possible that I am misunderstanding this challenge? Is it possible that I CAN do this? Is it possible that I don't actually need to do this? Is it possible that I am not giving myself enough credit? Etc.*

Another valuable secret I've learned is the importance of taking *imperfect* action. It's easy to get caught up in planning and preparation, but at some point, you have to take that first step toward your goals - and often, it needs to be messy. That can be scary, but it's essential if you want to achieve success.

I teach, perform, and incorporate *improv* into everything I do. If you are unfamiliar, improv (short for improvisation) is the art of saying *Yes! And...* to life. It's the art of accepting whatever comes your way with a collaborative energy. It's overriding your fear of the unknown and leveraging the present moment to see opportunities instead of obstacles.

When it comes to success, I can't tell you a single thing I've achieved *without* harnessing improv. It is literally in the DNA of my life. So sign up for an improv class, and get into the habit of saying *Yes! And...* to your ideas, instincts, and intuition. Yes! It is about accepting. And...is about taking action!

I always tell my clients to break their goals down into smaller, actionable steps. That way, they can focus on making daily progress rather than getting overwhelmed by the big picture. This allows them to instinctively take action every single day.

But, taking action isn't just about making progress toward your goals. It's also about building momentum and creating a positive feedback loop. When you take action and see results, it boosts your confidence and motivates you to keep going.

One of the tools I use to help my clients take action is accountability. You're more likely to follow through on your commitments when you're accountable to someone else. That's why I encourage my clients to find an accountability partner, whether it's a friend, family member, or coach.

Another valuable secret I've learned is the power of REAL networking. I'm sure you've heard *Success isn't about what you know, but who you know.* I will take this a step further and say it's about HOW you know WHO you know. It's quality over quantity. Most people suck at networking because they make it all about them. The secret is to find the commonalities between you and others (potential collaborators, mentors, clients, or even friends) and put the focus on them. People remember how you made them feel, not what you said. Building a strong network of REAL connections can open up doors and opportunities that you never thought possible.

When it comes to success, I can't tell you a single thing I've achieved *without* harnessing *genuine connections.* How do you have genuine conversations with people? See "Yes! And.." above.

That's why I always tell my clients to approach networking with a servant's heart. When you're focused on serving others and making a difference, success will follow.

Now, I want to return to something I said earlier in the chapter. "*...and also led me to realize that this wealth and success doesn't really matter as much as I thought it did.*"

Success is not just about achieving your goals. It's also about living a fulfilling and meaningful life. It's about understanding one core element of life. This is definitely a success secret. You (and everyone else) are only ever after a *feeling*. Think about it: everything you've ever wanted, or currently want, has to do with how you want to feel when you have it. Why do you want a 6-figure business? You want to feel content. You want to feel free. You want to feel powerful, unlimited, or happy. The truth is you are looking to your business to reach the height of these feelings. The deeper truth is you have to realize that those feelings are accessible right now within you. You cannot attract your biggest dreams unless you first become the person who matches them. Read that again twice.

If you've been spinning your wheels, as I did in the early days of my biz, chances are you are not showing up in the world as the highest version/vision of yourself.

We only ever attract what we *are*. Not what we *want*. That's why I always encourage my clients to identify their core values and priorities and build their goals and action steps around them.

When you are living a life aligned with your values and priorities, you'll feel fulfilled and happy, no matter what challenges come your way. But you must know what your top core values actually are. Most of us only think we know what is truly important to us.

Chances are, most of those things are *shoulds*. We often *should focus on* ourselves because we often make decisions and take actions based on *insecurities, insufficiencies, influences, or intellect -* instead of *intuition, instincts, inner-knowing, and innovation.*

This leads us to want things we don't truly want - because we fear we are not enough without these things. The truth is you are enough exactly as you are. So, from this place, ask yourself, *what is truly important to me?* This question can lead to questions like: *If I wasn't afraid of failure, what would I truly desire?*

Through questions like this, you will find your keywords like FREEDOM, CONNECTION, COMMUNITY, EQUALITY, etc. These are core values. These are the values you want to connect with inside of you each day. Want freedom? Find freedom within you first. Then, look for freedom around you. Then, more freedom comes your way. It really is that simple.

As I reflect on my constantly shifting journey to success, I realize that it was not just about the strategies and tactics I used but how I started each day.

Business, like everything else, is an inside job. That's why I became a certified NLP practitioner and integrated those techniques into my life and coaching practice.

One of the key principles of NLP is the idea that the meaning of communication is the response you get. In other words, if you are not getting the results you want, it's not because of the other person, it is because of how you're communicating (or not communicating).

Using NLP techniques, I help my clients communicate more effectively and get the results they want in their personal and professional lives.

A valuable NLP technique is anchoring. Anchoring is the process of associating a particular emotion or state with a physical trigger. For example, you might anchor a feeling of confidence to a particular hand gesture, so whenever you need a boost of confidence, you can make that gesture and access that feeling.

I use anchoring with my clients to help them access positive emotions and states whenever they need them. For example, suppose a client is feeling anxious about an upcoming presentation. In that case, I might anchor a feeling of calm and confidence to a particular word or phrase so that they can access that state during the presentation.

But, NLP is not just about techniques and strategies. It's also about understanding and working with your unconscious mind. Your unconscious mind is responsible for your beliefs, values, and habits, and it's often the source of self-sabotage and limiting beliefs. This is also why improv is so effective. It taps into your unconscious mind. It helps to override your nervous system's fear responses so you can think and act with clarity.

But it's important to remember that improv and NLP are not magic bullets. They are simply powerful practices of self-discovery and personal growth, and it takes time and effort to see real results. And that is why I want to share a very valuable (maybe the most valuable) success secret that I have learned (and continue to learn). And that is getting comfortable in the quiet. Sometimes, this manifests as sitting into frustration. Breathing through the endless waiting. Not being afraid of being alone. These are all things I continue to learn again and again. It's when I get quiet that I finally have clarity.

That's why I always tell my clients to be patient and persistent. Success is not a destination, it's a journey, and the most successful people are the ones who never give up.

I'm honored to be able to share my knowledge and experience with you in this chapter, and I hope that it has inspired you to take action toward your goals and dreams.

One of the commitments that I encourage my clients to develop is the commitment to gratitude. And yes, it IS a commitment because it is one of the first things to go when shit hits the fan. You must commit to it - like you'd commit to a romantic partner (brownie points for committing to gratitude WITH a partner as well). By focusing on the things that they are grateful for each day, my clients are able to shift their mindset from one of lack and scarcity to one of abundance and possibility. This shift in perspective can have a powerful impact on their overall well-being and success.

This needs to also lead to self-care. Many people neglect their own needs in the pursuit of success, but the truth is that taking care of yourself is essential to achieving your goals. That's why I encourage my clients (as well as myself) to prioritize their physical, emotional, and mental health - and to make self-care a non-negotiable part of their daily routine.

Of course, developing new habits and routines is not always easy. It takes time and effort to create lasting change. But, with the right mindset and strategies, it is possible.

Ultimately, success and leadership are about taking ownership of your life and your choices. It's about recognizing that you have the power to create the life that you want and taking action toward that vision. By developing their leadership skills, my clients are able to step into their full potential and achieve greater success and fulfillment in all areas of their lives.

As I reflect on my own journey towards success and self-empowerment, I am grateful for the lessons that I have learned along the way. From my experiences as an awkward gay teen with ADHD, my work as a filmmaker and actor, to my current role as a coach and motivational speaker, I have gained valuable insights into what it takes to overcome challenges and achieve unlimited wealth and success.

My message to anyone who is struggling to achieve their goals or find their purpose is this: You are capable of achieving unlimited wealth and success. You have within you the power to create the life that you truly want. With the right mindset, habits, and strategies, anything is possible.

My journey to becoming a 6-figure business coach hasn't been easy, but it's been worth it. I've learned the power of passion, purpose, and mindset, as well as the value of NLP and improv, and I've used this knowledge to help countless clients achieve their goals and live their best lives.

I hope this chapter has been insightful and inspiring for you. Remember, you have the

I hope this chapter has inspired you to pursue your dreams and live your best life. But above all, I hope that it reminded you of 1 key thing. You already have everything inside of you to be a successful 6-figure coach, and there is nothing this book can give you that isn't already there. How awesome is that?

Amanda Rose

Master Your Mind and You'll Master Your Life.

I never expected to become an entrepreneur. However, I always had grandiose dreams for my future. I grew up enamored by movie stars and pop stars, with dreams of becoming one of them and living out my life as a famous millionaire, living in grandiose mansions with beautiful sports cars and all the luxuries life has to offer. I'd use our fancy 5-CD-changer in the living room to perform imaginary concerts.

From as far back as I can remember, I knew that my purpose in this life was to shift the way people think so that they could live lives they loved. It was utterly baffling to me why people spent most of their lives working mundane soul-sucking jobs instead of chasing after their dreams, and I knew it was my job to awaken them to this. Back then, I assumed I'd accomplish this through art.

I was great in school, a steady honor roll A-student. Things just came naturally to me. I was also a high achiever because I knew I had ambitious dreams, and I wasn't going to let anything stand in my way of achieving them. I took music lessons for years as extra-curricular. I was wholly dedicated, but I made one big mistake: I bought into the lie that if you show up, do your best in school, and get good grades, then everything you ever wanted would be waiting for you on the other side… it certainly wasn't.

I was obsessed with my dreams, but I had one mountain of an obstacle in front of me: I wanted to be a rich and famous actor and singer, but I was obese. However, there wasn't anything I would let stand in my way. When I was 15 years old, I committed to losing weight, no matter what. This started as a full-throttle diet with intense exercising, but this quickly spiraled into full-blown anorexia. It ravaged my mind and my body. I lost 138 pounds by starving myself to the point where you could count my ribs, for about 16 months. They call it an eating disorder, but that's like calling depression a suicide disorder; anorexia is a mental illness, and I'd spend over a decade healing from the self-inflicted trauma and self-loathing.

In high school, I did all-day theatre in my last two years. Then, I went to Humber College in Toronto and enrolled in Acting for Film and Television, where I graduated with the Governor General's Award. I even landed a reputable agent from my work on our final film project in college. This all amounted to... almost nothing in the real world.

I graduated in 2008. When I graduated, the biggest recession since the great depression hit, and I was in for a rude awakening. Canadian film production heavily relies on US projects, but in 2008, for the first time in a very long time, the Canadian Dollar was stronger than the US dollar, so they weren't coming to film up here. There were next-to-no auditions to ever go to. Add to that, businesses, in general, were doing layoffs en masse, not hiring. This A-student, with honors and awards, couldn't even get a basic minimum-wage retail job.

After about a year, I finally got a job… door-to-door sales. Not exactly the life I'd envisioned for myself. Not by a long shot. I worked this job and eventually got a minimum-wage retail job as the economy was recovering. Auditions started cropping up, albeit infrequently. In 2010, there was a glimmer of hope. I booked a national commercial and a one-liner on a Canadian comedy. It gave me a glimmer of hope that my dreams weren't lost.

I ended up working for a company that only hired actors because they did live in-store sales presentations that were 30 minutes long and required script memorization, presenting skills, and some flare. I loved that job and threw myself fully into it. I was actually great at it too. They promoted me to be a sales trainer for new hires, and I loved that even more. Unfortunately, there was a huge management shift after a while, and it killed that job for me. Add to that, the travel time and work hours were insane, and I wanted to come back to my dreams and live life on my own terms.

I quit, with no plan, in June 2013. I had a few months of savings in my account and was getting married in September of that year. I needed to figure my shit out and fast. I was a homebody and wanted to stay at home, but I didn't have any ideas for a business of my own. I joined a Network Marketing Company that I'd been a customer of for years. It allowed me to use my sales skills without needing to come up with something to sell.

Selling online on social media is much different than selling in a store. People go into a store to shop but come on social media because they're bored, lonely, or want to share something.

Learning how to pivot and connect with people in a digital framework was excruciating. In my first year, I made a whopping $600. Year two, about $2000. Year three, about $3500. My growth was painfully slow. I worked my ass off and was dedicated to figuring it out, no matter how long it took. I knew there was no way in hell I'd ever go to work for anyone else, ever again.

In 2016, my husband came home from work midday and handed me a letter that said he'd been fired. In that moment, my blood turned to ice, and a knot formed in my stomach. At the time, I was earning about $600-1000 a month, certainly not enough for us to live on. It was as if time froze, and I saw two very clear roads in front of me: on one side, it was the path to figuring out how to file for bankruptcy, and on the other side, it was me finally figuring out my money shit. I chose the second path.

I got my hands on every book on mindset, manifesting, and wealth that I could. I devoured them, embodied them, and applied their action steps no matter how uncomfortable they were. I knew this was my last chance.

Immediately, small shifts happened… for the first time since I'd become an entrepreneur, suddenly, people were reaching out to me inquiring about my products and services. I was getting traction online. I was making sales with much more ease.

Still, it was a tumultuous time. It was a huge test of faith. Despite how dire things seemed, I surrendered to the process and believed it would all unfold in the best way for my greater good. After 6-months of dedicating myself to the Law of Attraction, deep mindset work, and healing my money wounds, we manifested over 6-figures, which was utterly life-changing. After nearly a decade of living under the poverty line, it was like winning the lottery!

We moved into a new house in 2017. I decided it was time to revive my lifelong dream of becoming a published author, so I pulled out the sci-fi manuscript I'd written when I was 16 and began editing it while also studying how to publish and market books. Simultaneously, after such a life-changing transformation, I knew my purpose in life was to bring the principles I'd learned about manifestation to the masses, so I began creating my first Law of Attraction course.

In the summer of 2018, I published my first book; I turned my Law of Attraction program into a book called *Manifesting on Purpose*. I chose to publish this book first because I wanted to "test run" publishing a book before publishing my science fiction novel, which meant so much to me. Ironically, to this day, *Manifesting on Purpose* has remained my number one bestselling book, and it has changed innumerable lives! Years later, as I worked to develop freebie-opt-ins to build my mailing list, I experienced this again: the simple things I had not even planned on making ended up being the highest converters. We often tend to think and work too hard on things when, really, simplicity wins the day.

I proceeded to publish my sci-fi book, *Fire Fury Freedom.* Then, I wrote a collection of short stories, as well as literary fiction, and then I wrote another book on Manifesting. I was hooked! From that, I started getting inquiries from other writers who wanted to know how to get published. This led to the creation of a 3-week program, *The Get Published Workshop.*

I shifted into business, mindset, manifesting, and wealth coaching in 2018. Since then, I've created over 40 programs and masterclasses, and published over 20 books, many of which are bestsellers. I've also been featured in magazines, on TV, in podcasts, and on blogs. I founded my corporation, *The Infinite Power of You Inc.*, in 2019, then started a podcast called the *No BS Biz Show* with a high-school friend, Tony Babcock, in 2020, and then in 2021, co-founded a corporation with him, the *No BS Biz Co. Ltd.* In 2022, I became a self-made millionaire.

As you can see, one thing led to the next and then the next. Opportunities arise all around us once we get into motion, and we can begin to create momentum. Much like a train, it's slow to get started, but once it picks up momentum, it can ram through any obstacle and keep going!

The truth is you can accomplish anything you set your mind to. There isn't anything that you cannot achieve if you wholly commit to doing so. Everything existence started as just a thought because it took physical form. You get to design your reality! *Let's dig into how...*

Success Secrets

1. **MASTER YOUR MIND AND YOU MASTER YOUR LIFE**
2. **FOCUS**
3. **HABITS**

Did you enjoy reading **SIX FIGURE SUCCESS SECRETS VOL. 1?**

If so, we would be grateful if you took a moment to leave a review on Amazon to help other readers find this book!

Thank you!

ABOUT THE AUTHORS

Nicole Cherie Hesse

Unicorn Client Attraction Coach

Nicole Cherie Hesse, CEO of Unicorn Attraction, has empowered thousands of entrepreneurs to attract unicorn clients without the struggle of cold outreach using energetically aligned social selling strategies.

From bartender to 7-figure CEO in just 13 months, Nicole has repositioned her skill sets and colorful life experience to create a movement. In overcoming abuse, loss, and grief, Nicole has a unique perspective on the world of sales. She stands firmly against pain point tactics and uses her signature strategy of catalyst Marketing to attract her unicorn clients.

Nicole helps her clients align their offers and use their personal stories, trials, and tribulations to dominate their industries. Nicole's Clients have gone on to make 5 and even 6-figures a month using her proven marketing system. Nicole is currently writing a fiction novel based on events from her past. She has a podcast called Real Unicorns Don't Wear Pants, where she shares her stories and strategies for creating a successful online coaching business.

Grab Nicole's Amazing Free Gift for You:
www.NonstopNotifications.com

Join Nicole's Facebook Group: https://www.facebook.com/groups/wonderwomenthrive/

For Media Inquiries See Nicole's Press Kit:
https://www.canva.com/design/DAFPiubXagE/CKRwn1q0moDgsvPe-dTAWA/view

Richard Blakely

Richard is a successful business leader with almost 40 years of I.T. industry experience. He believes in paying it forward and random acts of kindness – love your life.

If You'd like to Send a Message to Richard, please e-mail your message to Amanda at <u>amanda@theinfinitepowerofyou.com</u> and your message will be forwarded to him.

Sarah Lines

 Sarah Lines helps soul-driven, spiritual entrepreneurs on a mission to delete old paradigms, to more deeply connect with their inner being, and activate their purpose.

As a Soul-Life-Biz Alchemist and channel, Sarah leads visionary women into superconscious creation to manifest the life and business of their dreams, catapulting them into a new energy of radiance, abundance, and purpose-driven lives.

With lifetimes of experience, she has helped hundreds of clients awaken, ascend, and powerfully create new realities. Creator of the Goddess Alchemy Academy, Sarah has authored multiple books, including international best sellers.

Visit:

www.facebook.com/SoulfulSarahLines

Amy Lewis

Nothing inspires Amy more than helping determined entrepreneurs connect deeply with themselves, gain clarity, and create consistent cash flow without sacrificing their health or their relationships.

Amy spent over two decades in the fitness business industry. She built multiple 6-figure businesses and helped others do the same in a variety of industries, in addition to consulting with multiple 6-and-7-figure businesses to simplify operations and increase impact and income while changing the workplace/world culture.

With a strong background in sales and marketing, Amy generated award-winning sales to the tune of over a million dollars in less than nine months.

Amy has a passion for helping determined entrepreneurs deeply connect with themselves to create consistent cash flow month over month, quickly, so that they are connected to something greater than themselves, feel supported, and can meet and exceed their goals and instigate true change.

She understands that how you do anything is how you do everything, which is exactly why the connection with self is so important.

Amy strives to grow her business with the same integrity, communication, and collaboration that she and her team use with their clients to encourage compassion, expansion, and real results for all.

Website:

www.fusionfitnessvt.com

Social Media:

www.facebook.com/groups/strongbeautifulu/

www.facebook.com/amy.dabrush.lewis/

www.facebook.com/fusionfitnessvt/

www.instagram.com/amylewissolutions

Allison Barnett

Allison Barnett is the CEO and Founder of BRG Unlimited LLC., a premier Luxury Real Estate Agent, Channeler, Energy Shifter, and Manifestation and Business Coach. Her practice is rooted in spirituality, offering a unique blend of energetic mastery and industry experience to create magic with her clients.

Taking an unconventional approach to business that includes intuitive guidance and manifestation techniques, Allison built her career upon the foundation of a Juris Doctorate cum Laude from John Marshall Law School and a Bachelor of Science in Communications and

Broadcasting from the University of Tennessee. She then carved a niche for herself as an Intuitive Realtor experienced in new construction, sales management, design, luxury, coaching, and more.

Allison appeared on *The Negotiators,* a Reveel Entertainment original series, for her *I-Buyer* knowledge. She was also featured in *Top Agent Magazine* and *The Mortgage Reports,* as well as guest appearances on various podcasts. Allison has received numerous awards and recognitions, including an appointment to the launch team for *Hoodle,* being named *Best of Woodstock,* and continued membership in the *MultiMillion Dollar Club.*

Focused on helping clients navigate their next moves, personally and professionally, Allison continues to practice real estate while mentoring agents and business owners to manifest and uplevel, locally and abroad. In addition, she produces her own YouTube channel, *The Allison*

Barnett Show, co-creates for the Craig and Alli brand, and collaborates with her husband, Knox, on joint business ventures.

Visit: *AllisonBarnett.live* for offers and opportunities to make magic happen with Allison.

Sherice Kral

Sherice Kral is uniquely qualified to help hard-working entrepreneurs who are focused on achieving success to unlock their wildest dreams.

As a Certified Maxwell Leadership Coach, International Keynote Speaker, and Certified Robbins-Madanes Trained Strategic Intervention Coach, Kral has the experience and expertise to guide entrepreneurs to the success they strive for. With 10 years of service in the U.S. Army and years of successful consulting experience with Fortune 500 companies, Sherice is dedicated to helping entrepreneurs reach their goals. Her impressive track record includes founding the

American Club Association's Master Coach Endorsement Certification and growing dozens of memberships an average of 533% within three months. Follow Sherice Kral on social media to discover how she can help you gain radical clarity and honesty through the ocean of online business, marketing, and mindset needs.

Visit:

https://www.thrivingentrepreneurs.org/

Tony Babcock

Tony Babcock is the CEO and Founder of The Present You Inc., Co-Founder of No BS Biz Co. Ltd., Co-Host of the No BS Biz Show Podcast, a Certified Life Coach, a NLP Practitioner, an Author, and a Motivational Speaker.

He has worked with over 1500 Creative Entrepreneurs and some of the world's largest companies, inspiring lasting change and growth from the inside out. He is also a professional actor, TV Host, and Entrepreneur with three successful businesses.

His Company, The Present You Inc., is all about infusing authenticity with strategy so you can tap into your inner creative and build a biz that is passion-filled and profitable!

We serve a community of passionate, driven entrepreneurs (mainly coaches, trainers, healers, and leaders) and help them create, nurture, and scale an exciting, focused business - all while being themselves, channeling their creativity, and stopping to smell the roses.

Visit:

https://www.thepresentyouinc.com/

Amanda Rose

Amanda Rose is the CEO and founder of The Infinite Power of You INC., Co-Founder of No BS Biz Co. Ltd., Self-Made Millionaire, Co-Host of the No BS Biz Show Podcast, a Business, Wealth and Mindset Coach, Multi-Published Multi-Genre Author, Motivational Speaker, Course Creator, and Actor.

Her corporation serves entrepreneurs worldwide, with her unique approach that focuses on understanding each client's individual strengths and guiding them in building their own methodology rather than attempting to get them to adapt to a specific mold.

Amanda has been a sales expert for over a decade, having experience in door-to-door sales, retail, live sales presentation, network marketing, and online product and service sales, which allows her to bring extensive insight to her clients. Amanda has been featured in many publications and news articles for her work, including **FOX, CBS,** Yahoo! Finance, and **NBC,** and was recently recognized with the BRAINZ Global 500 Award and the CREA 2021 Award. Amanda passionately works to help entrepreneurs succeed through her corporation as well as within her Facebook Community.

Visit:

https://amanda-rose.mykajabi.com/